Dearest Friend,
When I read the first few pages of this little book, I instantly thought of you and I and the way we feel about our boys.

Merry Christmas to all the Peales

Love
Sherron

Although
The Day Is Not Mine To Give,
I'LL SHOW YOU
THE MORNING
SUN

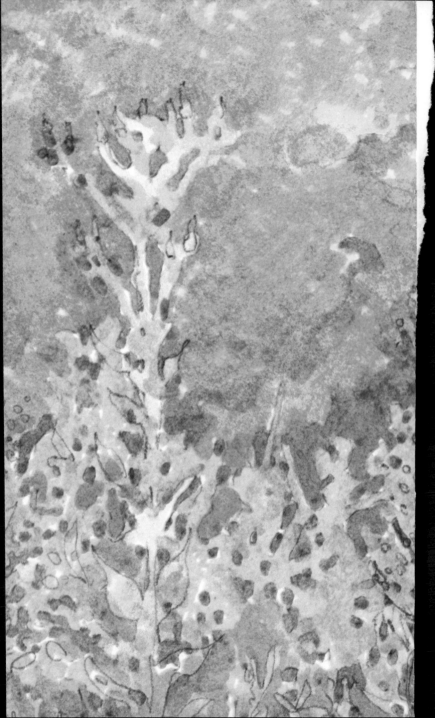

Although *The* Day Is Not Mine To Give, I'LL SHOW YOU THE *MORNING* SUN

Written and Illustrated
by
David Melton

STANYAN BOOKS

RANDOM HOUSE

A Stanyan Book
Published by Stanyan Books,
8721 Sunset Blvd., Suite C
Los Angeles, California 90069,
and by Random House, Inc.
201 E. 50th Street,
New York, New York 10022

Library of Congress
Catalog Card Number: 76-160144

Designed by David Melton

Printed in U.S.A.

For
Traci and Todd

The Morning Sun

My child,
my child,
your days of childhood
are quickly spent.
As the season passes,
I wonder why
it hurries so.

I look from the window
to watch you playing
in the yard,
your bird's nest hair,
disarranged
by changing winds,
and carefree days.
Your sun-toasted face
peers from beneath
your tousled thatch.
Quick, darting looks
clear your vision;
I see you
dream your dreams.

My backyard vagabond —
collecting dirt samples
under your nails,
both fingers and toes,
as you roam
your private domain,
shimmying up tree trunks,
exploring leafed branches,
and burrowing through
a spread of bushes.

Castle towers
loom in your mind.
Outer space
revolves within.
Chart your jungle trails,
Amazons of imaginary rivers,
stopping only for
peanut butter sandwiches
and dinner calls.

Tonight,
tell-tale rings
will decorate the tub,
and discarded clothes
will be dropped,
and probably left
in a heap,
on the floor.

Scrubbed,
and hair combed,
you'll emerge,
clean and shining,
without a remaining trace
of the day's adventures —
except for the lights
in your sky-clear eyes.

After your bath,
wrapped in clean softness,
you will sleep
in the quiet of the night.

I have never counted the hours
that I have listened to
evening prayers,
nor the times
I have walked into your room
to straighten your covers,
or just watch as you sleep.

Sometimes,
I stand in the quiet
and listen
to the sounds of your breathing.
I find myself
remembering
a smaller you —
a tiny hand reaching out
from cotton blankets
to search for the world.
Sometimes, your little fingers
wedged between my lips
to feel a kiss
tighten around them.

Other times,
waving your hands,
you watched the light
dance between
your fingers,
as the sun
plays hide and seek
through the leaves
of windblown branches.

The same small hand
learned to wave goodbye
and offer anxious greeting.
It learned to wrap around my thumb,
to clutch rattles
and building blocks,
and to search pockets
for questionable treasures.

It was too soon
for pencils
and scissors.
Their turn came later.

Roller skates
came packaged in boxes
with skinned knees.
Wagons,
brightly painted,
brought scraped shins
and mashed toes.
Bicycles chewed elbows and knees.
Car doors bit your fingers.
Shaggy rugs stumbled your toes.
Waxed floors slipped
beneath unsure feet.
And open drawers
gave sudden bangs
to your head,
toes,
and all points between.

Sometimes,
I wonder
where the time has gone;
and where it is going.
Sand sifts the minutes,
cogs tick away the seconds,
allowing little time
for recollection.

So little time
from tricycles to bicycles,
between trips to the orthodontist,
and the hours which television
holds us captive.

I find myself,
saying to myself,
"If I had it to live again,
somehow I'd grab the moments;"
not considering,
I'm letting others slip away
while I think about it.
Too many things to steal our attention:
The washing machine must be fed,
and the car needs repair again.

I hope that
in these years,
I have attended
to more than skinned knees
and cut fingers.
I hope that somewhere,
in the everyday,
that I have not overlooked
the needs of your heart,
and the growth of your spirit.
I hope that somewhere
in the while,
there was enough
worth the while.

And if there was not . . .
and if there was not . . .
and if there was not . . .
I don't know now
how I can make it up to you.

Yesterday,
you asked beautiful questions:
Why is the grass green?
How did the little man
get inside the TV?

And . . .
What does God look like?

Today,
you ask the questions
of a probing mind:
What is the distance to the sun?
Why does the lightning flash?

And . . .
Where does God live?

Tomorrow,
I know there will be more questions.
Some, I am not eager to hear.
And some I'll be unable to answer:
Why is the sky a polluted gray?
Why are the rivers turning black?
Why are there still wars?

And . . .
Is there really a God?

Sometimes,
I find myself
regarding you
as a miniature adult;
not tall enough
to be rewarded respect,
not subtle enough
to be offered consideration.
I give you love
as I might offer you
a slice of cake.
Enough, perhaps,
to entice your taste
and encourage your appetite,
but not sufficient
to nourish your needs.

The miracle is not
that you grow
with my love.
The miracle is that
you seem to survive
my mistakes.

I shall not ask the wind
what storm it carries,
or ask the earth
what rocks it bares.
I shall not ask the sky
what stars will fall.
I will be content
to let the wind
carry its burden,
and to let the earth
endure its own.
And I will let the sky
be concerned with
its wayward stars.

I will busy myself
watching over my own children.
I leave the universe
in better prepared
and more competent hands.

I tell you fairytales
as long as you listen.
I build castles in your mind
as long as you permit.
I sing you lullabies
as long as you dream.
I teach you words,
that·you might express
new and adventurous thoughts
of your own.
I give you love

to nourish your spirit.
I teach you to read
to enlighten your mind,
knowing that knowledge
will lead you
to unexplored corridors
over which
I have no control.

Too soon,
the same words
which will lead you
to Milton,
Thoreau,
and Shakespeare,
will also take you
to the headlines in
the daily news.

As I fill your
days of childhood
with Christmas carols and fairytales,
I must also
prepare you for realities.
I must offer you both —
the way the world should be
and the way it is.
Introducing both
may tend to confuse,
but ignoring either
would only cheat you of Life.

Although the day is not mine to give,
I'll show you the morning sun.
We will walk
through fields unexplored,
and wander streets
you have yet to see.

We will walk,
hand in hand,
as thousands have walked
before us.
We'll make believe
that only the wind
has touched the leaves,
and only the rain
has felt the earth.

We'll watch,
together,
as a bird
circles a cloudless sky,
in constant search
for morsels of food
to feed her young.

We will listen,
you and I,
for the rippling sounds
of a wandering brook.
Together,
we will follow
the bends of its gentle course.

Take my hand, my child,
and we will
explore the land.
I will tell you
all that I know,
and you will show me
the secrets of the heart.
It may not be a fair exchange,
but it is all that I have to give.

In Spring,
we will find
a meadow green.
We'll touch new-forming buds,
and share the wonder
they have in store.

In Summer,
we will cross
seas of grass,
observing signposts —
but we'll determine
our own direction.

In Fall,
we will become
a part of the changing colors,
and feel fallen leaves
crackle beneath our feet.

In Winter,
we will face the wind,
and plant our footsteps
in the pathless snow.
We will know the seasons,
becoming a part of them,
as they become a part of us.

I will watch over you
as you blossom
and take on
new forms of awareness.
A part of Nature,
not removed;
a necessary segment
of the overall design —
an element
in the pattern.

I shall lead you
for only this short while,
not knowing
whether or not
you are to become
one,
in the formation
of even rows of Mankind;
or if you are to become
one,
and alone;
an individual
to create a new course
for others to follow.

How can I find
appropriate words
that say only the right things?
How can I find
proper answers
to answer
the questions you ask?
How can I lead you
when I, myself,
am in need of guidance?
How can I be a parent
when much of me
is still a child?
As I learn to understand you,
perhaps you, in turn,
will learn to understand me.

I warm your hand
in the warmth of my own.
My touch
encourages you to touch.
My voice tempers your voice.
My smile becomes your smile.
My anger, your anger.
My joy is your own.
And my fears are your fears.

In years to come,
I will see in you,
a reflection of myself.
It's a happy thought
when I understand,
and am in control
of my own attitudes.
It's an overpowering
and frightening thought
when I am not.

If winter comes,
we will look for shelter
and wait out the storm,
away from the outside
and the chilling winds.
I will protect you
from the dark,
and come morning,
I will show you the sun.

I will listen to your voice
and be warmed by its sound.
I will look into your eyes
and feel content.
I will touch your hand
and be comforted.
And these short years,
we will share,
together.

As you prepare
to chart new pathways
of your own,
when we come to the path
that only you can see,
or come to a hill
that only you can climb,
I promise not to hold you back.
Instead,
I will encourage you
to go on.

There will be
no goodbyes
for us —
no farewells.
For as you leave,
a part of my existence
will go with you,
and I shall not
again, be whole and complete
until you return.

The day a child is born
becomes a special date,
to be marked on calendars
and in the hearts of parents.
Age will be counted
with its return —
an occasion for gifts
and parties,
adorned with paper hats,
and candles standing
in formation,
on confectionery foam.
And soon,
too soon,
the primary numbers
become teens.
And soon,
too soon,
my child
is a child
no more.